AI Innovations: Transforming Industries and Lives

Aisha Khan

Copyright © [2023] by Aisha Khan

All rights reserved. No part of this publication may be reproduced, distributed, or transmitted in any form or by any means, including photocopying, recording, or other electronic or mechanical methods, without the prior written permission of the publisher, except in the case of brief quotations embodied in critical reviews and certain other noncommercial uses permitted by copyright law

Author: Aisha Khan

Title: AI Innovations: Transforming Industries and Lives

Cover design by Mr.Vinod

Interior layout and design by Mr. Salman

Disclaimer:
The views and opinions expressed in this book are those of the author and do not necessarily reflect the official policy or position of any other agency, organization, employer, or company. Assumptions made in the analysis are not reflective of the position of any entity other than the author.

ISBN: 978-93-5868-217-5

CONTENTS

Chapter 1: Introduction to AI and Its Impact   **05**
- ❖ An overview of artificial intelligence (AI) and its historical context.
- ❖ The rapid growth of AI in recent years and its transformative potential.
- ❖ A discussion of the book's purpose and what readers can expect to learn.

Chapter 2: The AI Revolution in Industry   **19**
- ❖ Exploring how AI is reshaping various industries, such as healthcare, finance, and manufacturing.
- ❖ Real-world case studies showcasing the impact of AI on business operations and efficiency.
- ❖ The challenges and opportunities presented by AI adoption in the corporate world.

Chapter 3: AI in Everyday Life   **34**
- ❖ How AI technologies are becoming an integral part of our daily lives.
- ❖ A look at AI-powered applications like virtual assistants, autonomous vehicles, and smart homes.
- ❖ Ethical and privacy concerns related to the pervasive use of AI in society.

Chapter 4: The Technology Behind AI   **47**
- ❖ An in-depth examination of the underlying technologies and algorithms that power AI systems.
- ❖ Machine learning, neural networks, deep learning, and natural language processing.
- ❖ The role of data and data collection in AI development.

Chapter 5: The Future of AI   **63**
- ❖ Predictions and trends for the future of AI innovation.

- ❖ The potential societal impacts and ethical considerations of advanced AI.
- ❖ The importance of responsible AI development and the need for regulation.

Conclusion   **77**

Chapter 1: Introduction to AI and Its Impact

An overview of artificial intelligence (AI) and its historical context

Introduction

Artificial intelligence (AI) is the study and development of computer systems capable of performing activities normally requiring human intelligence. Among these are such activities as linguistic comprehension, pattern recognition, problem solving, and experiential learning. Scientists, academics, and the general public alike have become fascinated by the idea of AI, which has led to tremendous technological advances. From its origins in ancient mythology to its applications in cutting-edge AI research today, this essay presents a comprehensive review of the field.

Myths and Theories from the Past

Ancient cultures and mythologies frequently feature artificial entities with human-level intellect. Hephaestus, the Greek deity of blacksmiths and craftspeople, was able to accomplish much more with the help of his mechanical workers. Similar accounts of automata and artificial birds that may pass for human are found in ancient Chinese and Egyptian writings. These early ideas paved the way for the modern interest with building artificially intelligent devices.

When Artificial Intelligence Began: Alan Turing and the Turing Test

The seminal work of British mathematician and logician Alan Turing in the middle of the 20th century marked the beginning of the contemporary era of artificial intelligence. To assess whether or not a machine is capable of intelligent behavior that is indistinguishable from that of a person, Turing developed a test in 1950. The Turing Test is an important notion in the history of artificial intelligence. Interest in creating machines that could mimic human mind was aroused by Turing's ideas.

Expert Systems and the Coming "AI Winter"
Expert systems were made possible by breakthroughs in artificial intelligence research in the 1960s and 1970s. These programs have the ability to tackle difficult problems and offer insightful analysis since they were developed to emulate human competence in specific subjects. However, the initial euphoria surrounding AI dissipated in the 1980s due to false expectations, technical constraints, and a lack of financing. The AI winter was a temporary lull in the progress of AI studies.

The Explosion of Neural Networks and Machine Learning
Improvements in machine learning and neural networks sparked a revival of interest in AI in the latter part of the 20th century. To enable computers to learn from data, recognize patterns, and make predictions without explicit programming, machine learning algorithms were developed. Inspired by the structure of the human brain, neural networks became an essential part in creating advanced AI systems that can do tasks such as image identification and natural language processing.

Deep Learning and Big Data, Two Trends in Modern AI
Deep learning algorithms have had a dramatic impact on the field of artificial intelligence in recent years. When applied to large datasets, deep learning models—and in particular deep neural networks—can extract valuable insights. The availability of large datasets for use in preparing AI models for use has been greatly facilitated by big data technology. As a result of the synergy between deep learning and big data, AI has been catapulted to new heights, opening the door to

developments like self-driving cars, customized suggestions, and accurate medical diagnoses.

AI's Social and Ethical Consequences
There are moral and social issues to consider as AI develops. Responsible development and deployment of AI systems has been the subject of heated debate due to concerns over privacy, algorithmic bias, and the impact on jobs. Ethical rules and laws for AI are now being developed by researchers and legislators to maximize the technology's positive effects on society and mitigate any negative ones.

Tendencies and Future Challenges
Several novel developments and difficulties are shaping the future of AI. The advent of quantum computing has the potential to accelerate the solution of difficult AI problems, paving the way for groundbreaking new discoveries and innovations. Moreover, AI's integration with other developing technologies like robots, IoT, and AR is anticipated to produce novel applications in a wide range of sectors.

However, there are still significant obstacles to overcome, such as assuring AI fairness and openness, resolving cybersecurity concerns, and encouraging interdisciplinary collaboration. In order to effectively handle these issues, interdisciplinary techniques that combine knowledge from areas like as computer science, psychology, ethics, and the social sciences are required.

Conclusion
The concept of artificial intelligence has progressed significantly from its mythological origins. From the visionary ideas of Alan Turing to the creation of expert systems, machine learning, and deep neural networks, AI has evolved into a transformative technology with numerous applications.

Even as progress is being made in artificial intelligence, questions of ethics and societal impact continue to be at the forefront of scientists' minds.

Developing and deploying AI in the future requires a cautious and responsible approach. The entire potential of AI may be used for social good provided we address ethical problems, encourage interdisciplinary collaboration, and welcome novel approaches. When it comes to molding our present and defining the possibilities of our future, artificial intelligence (AI) was previously considered the domain of science fiction.

The rapid growth of AI in recent years and its transformative potential.

The development of artificial intelligence (AI) has exploded in popularity in recent years, influencing many spheres of society and disrupting markets around the world. Technological advancements in artificial intelligence (AI) have resulted from better algorithms, more powerful computers, and massive volumes of data. This article digs into what's behind AI's meteoric rise and what it could mean for the future of many different industries.

Innovations in Technology Fueling the Development of AI
Big Data, No. 1
The widespread availability and ease of access to large datasets is a key factor in the AI industry's meteoric rise. Everything from social media posts and online purchases to medical records and scientific findings have contributed to the massive data explosion of the digital age. Artificial intelligence systems feed off data, using it to learn, recognize patterns, and make predictions. The glut of big data has given a fertile field for AI applications, enabling the development of powerful machine learning models capable of performing complex tasks.

Enhanced Processing Capacity
The development of AI has been greatly helped by the increase in computational capacity. Powerful processors and graphics processing units (GPUs) are now capable of handling the massive computing needs of AI algorithms. The democratization of high-performance computing resources made possible by cloud computing services has allowed academics, developers, and companies to experiment with and implement AI systems without making costly upfront hardware investments. Because of this ease of access, AI

solutions have been developed and deployed more quickly across sectors.

Third, Developments in Algorithms for Machine Learning
Advances in machine learning—a branch of artificial intelligence—have been made possible by new algorithms and methods. In the field of artificial intelligence, deep learning, a branch of machine learning based on neural networks, has been a game-changer. Inspired by the structure of the human brain, deep neural networks excel in tasks such as image recognition, natural language processing, and speech recognition because of their ability to handle large volumes of data and extract complex patterns. The ever-increasing sophistication of these algorithms has allowed AI to penetrate several fields that were once thought inaccessible to it.

The Potential Revolutionary Impact of AI Technologies
1) Medical Care
The use of AI in healthcare has the potential to significantly improve diagnosis, treatment planning, and overall patient care. Medical pictures, such as X-rays and MRIs, can be analyzed by machine learning algorithms with surprising accuracy, helping doctors make early diagnoses of diseases and ailments. AI-powered predictive analytics can monitor public health data for signs of impending outbreaks, allowing for preventative steps to be taken. In addition, robotics and automation powered by AI are improving surgical operations by increasing precision and decreasing downtime.

Number Two: Money and Finances
Artificial intelligence (AI) technologies are transforming the finance industry. Algorithms driven by artificial intelligence can examine massive databases to spot fraudulent behaviors in real time, making financial transactions more secure. In order to maximize profits for investors, automated trading systems

employ artificial intelligence to forecast market movements and optimize investment portfolios. Furthermore, chatbots and virtual assistants with AI capabilities improve customer service by giving customers tailored advice and assistance.

3. Methods of Transport

The advent of driverless vehicles is only one example of how AI is propelling transportation forward. Camera, lidar, and radar data are processed by machine learning algorithms so that autonomous vehicles can drive themselves safely. These developments have the potential to reduce accidents, lower transportation costs, and increase mobility for those with disabilities. AI-powered optimization algorithms also boost traffic management systems, reducing congestion and improving the overall efficiency of transportation networks.

Learning #4.

Artificial intelligence technologies are having a profound impact on the educational landscape, improving outcomes for both students and teachers. Intelligent tutoring systems use adaptive algorithms to modify learning materials, responding to individual students' requirements and learning styles. Chatbots powered by AI help kids right now with things like questions and homework. In addition, AI-enhanced data analytics aid schools in monitoring student progress, pinpointing problem areas, and honing in on the most effective strategies for imparting knowledge.

Automated artificial intelligence (AI) systems are revolutionizing the manufacturing sector by boosting productivity, cutting costs, and enhancing product quality. Complex assembly-line operations are no match for robots endowed with artificial intelligence. Artificial intelligence (AI)-based predictive maintenance analyzes data from machines to foresee and prevent breakdowns and associated expenses.

AI-enabled "smart factories" improve manufacturing operations' adaptability to market needs by streamlining production, stock management, and supply-chain logistics.

6. Service to Customers

Artificial intelligence (AI)-powered chatbots and virtual assistants are reshaping customer service in several industries. Customer service is improved by these smart systems since they can answer questions, suggest products, and help solve issues. Natural language processing techniques enable chatbots to interpret and reply to consumer requests in real-time, ensuring rapid and efficient customer assistance. In order to maximize operational efficiency, organizations are increasingly turning to automation to free up workers for higher-order, more strategic duties.

Difficulties and Moral Concerns

It's important to address the challenges and ethical concerns raised by AI's rapid development, despite the many benefits it offers. One of the key issues is the possible bias in AI algorithms, which can perpetuate existing socioeconomic disparities and injustice. Prejudiced data used in training can have unintended consequences that disproportionately harm vulnerable populations. To reduce these discriminatory tendencies and advance equitable opportunity for all, it is crucial to implement fair and transparent AI systems.

Another major issue with AI is the potential invasion of privacy. Data privacy and security are of the utmost importance because AI systems rely so heavily on it. Robust regulatory and ethical frameworks are needed to strike a balance between leveraging data for AI applications and protecting individuals' privacy rights.

There are also worries about how AI will affect the job market. The possibility for specific vocations to be replaced by automation enabled by AI technology raises concerns about labor displacement and the necessity of upskilling and reskilling initiatives. Prepare the workforce for the new employment landscape brought on by AI with proactive steps including investing in education and training initiatives.

Conclusion

A new era of technological innovation and revolutionary potential has begun with the rapid growth of AI in recent years. Artificial intelligence technologies are altering industries all over the world, increasing efficiency and expanding the quality of services in fields as diverse as healthcare, finance, transportation, and education. AI is now in a position to take on previously insurmountable challenges thanks to the confluence of massive amounts of data, greater computational capacity, and sophisticated machine learning techniques.

As AI becomes more pervasive, however, it becomes more important than ever to address the difficulties and ethical concerns that come with implementing it. Trust among users and stakeholders can only be built if AI systems are fair, transparent, and protect user data. Additionally, upskilling and reskilling programs are essential to equip individuals with the tools they need to thrive in the face of automation.

To properly realize AI's transformational potential, society must carefully consider its ethical and societal ramifications. Using AI technology, we can promote a future where innovation and inclusion coexist for the benefit of individuals and communities by supporting responsible AI development, embracing interdisciplinary collaboration, and valuing human-centric values. The exponential development of AI is more than just a scientific breakthrough; it is a force for good that is reshaping the world into one that is more efficient, interconnected, and equal.

A discussion of the book's purpose and what readers can expect to learn

Artificial Intelligence (AI) is a game-changer in today's technological world, revolutionizing entire sectors and people's daily lives in unanticipated ways. The book "AI Innovations: Transforming Industries and Lives" examines the revolutionary potential of AI technologies across a variety of fields. Through this analysis, we will dissect the book's goals, themes, and what readers can take away from the book's illuminating pages.

Why This Book Was Written:
The goal of "AI Innovations: Transforming Industries and Lives" is to educate readers on the far-reaching effects of artificial intelligence technologies. The book's goal is to help lay people understand the complex world of AI innovation by providing a straightforward and comprehensible look at the topic. This book simplifies complex AI concepts and applications, allowing readers to better grasp the relevance of AI in the modern world.

The book begins by charting the development of artificial intelligence from its mythological beginnings to its conceptualization in the middle of the twentieth century and subsequent expansion into a transformational force. Readers will have a better grasp of the significance of recent AI advances if they have a firm grounding in the field's history.

Second, the book delves into the underlying ideas of AI and clarifies the most important parts of the field, such as machine learning, neural networks, deep learning, and natural language processing. These fundamental ideas are the backbone of cutting-edge applications, and understanding them will help readers better appreciate how AI systems learn, adapt, and make judgments.

Third, the book examines the effects of AI on a variety of industries, including medicine, banking, transportation, education, and manufacturing. Learn how AI technologies are streamlining processes, boosting efficiency, and generating extraordinary growth with examples and case studies from the real world.

Topics including algorithmic bias, data privacy, and the societal and economic impact of automation, all of which have ethical implications, are explored in the book. In order to better understand how to create and deploy AI systems in a responsible manner, readers are urged to critically evaluate the ethical challenges posed by technological advances in the field of AI.

Future Trends and Challenges: The book looks ahead to new trends in AI, such as quantum computing, human-AI collaboration, and ethical AI frameworks, and discusses their implications and potential applications. Additionally, it highlights the problems that lie ahead, including the need for interdisciplinary collaboration, resolving cybersecurity concerns, and providing equal access to AI advancements.

What the Reader Will Pick Up On 1. A Deep and Broad Knowledge of the Ideas Behind Artificial Intelligence
Machine learning algorithms, neural networks, and deep learning models are just some of the AI basics that will be covered in this book. The book helps readers make sense of AI advancements and their practical applications by simplifying these difficult issues.

Learn how AI is changing sectors like healthcare, banking, transportation, education, and manufacturing through in-depth case studies and examples. By looking at these real-world applications, readers can gain an understanding of how AI technologies are being put to use to boost productivity, refine decision-making, and fuel creativity in a wide range of industries.

3. Contemplation of Moral and Social Consequences: The book educates readers on the moral and societal implications of artificial intelligence. The effects of automation on society, data privacy, and other topics will be discussed. Readers are urged to participate in conversations on responsible AI development by critically engaging with AI breakthroughs after becoming familiar with these ethical dilemmas.

Readers may anticipate an examination of the future trends, such as quantum computing and human-AI collaboration, that are changing the AI environment. In addition, the book digs into the difficulties that innovators and policymakers in the AI space face, such as cyber security concerns and the unequal distribution of AI's benefits. A better understanding of the changing AI ecosystem and the preventative actions required for its long-term viability can be gained by looking ahead to these trends and obstacles.

Fifth, the book encourages readers to experiment with new ways of using AI in their own professions, leading to new opportunities for collaboration and innovation. Further, the book promotes a culture of creativity and information sharing by helping its readers appreciate the multidisciplinary nature of artificial intelligence.

In sum, "AI Innovations: Transforming Industries and Lives" is an excellent guide for those who want to learn more about this rapidly developing field. The book equips readers to embrace the transformational potential of AI technology by clarifying key principles, exploring industry-specific applications, addressing ethical considerations, and anticipating future trends. As they work through the book's material, readers get the understanding and perspective they need to take an active role in discussions about AI innovation, paving the way for a future in which AI continues to positively affect industries and people's daily lives.

Chapter 2: The AI Revolution in Industry

Exploring how AI is reshaping various industries, such as healthcare, finance, and manufacturing

Artificial intelligence (AI) has become a game-changing innovation across a wide range of sectors, dramatically changing the way in which products and services are produced and distributed. In recent years, AI technologies have received widespread adoption across industries, resulting in groundbreaking improvements in productivity, precision, and originality. This article explores how AI is changing the healthcare, financial, and manufacturing sectors. We can learn a great deal about the dramatic changes that AI is bringing to the corporate landscape by examining individual applications and the influence of AI in these areas.

First, Healthcare: How Big Data Is Changing Treatment and Diagnosis
Artificial intelligence (AI) is changing the face of healthcare by improving diagnosis and treatment. Thanks to machine learning algorithms fed by massive datasets, doctors can now make more precise diagnoses than ever before. In medicine, for example, AI can analyze X-rays, MRIs, and CT scans to spot abnormalities and spot diseases like cancer in their early stages. Artificial intelligence algorithms can analyze medical images far more quickly than humans can, allowing for more rapid diagnosis and treatment.

AI is also playing a crucial role in drug research and development. Artificial intelligence (AI) algorithms are being used by the pharmaceutical industry to analyze large amounts of biological data, speeding up the process of identifying new medication candidates. By predicting the efficacy and safety of new compounds, machine learning algorithms drastically cut down on the time and money normally spent on medication development. It is hoped that by streamlining the process, innovative therapies can be brought to patients more quickly, helping to meet unmet medical needs and improve healthcare outcomes.

In addition, chatbots and other AI-powered virtual health assistants are improving patient participation and comfort. Improve the patient experience and treatment plan adherence with the use of these smart technologies' ability to offer individualized health advice, prescription reminders, and mental health assistance. In addition, AI-powered predictive analytics allow healthcare facilities to better allocate their resources, anticipate illness outbreaks, and enhance their preventative care programs, all of which contribute to higher quality treatment at a lower cost to patients.

2.Money: Increasing Productivity and Delighting Customers
Artificial intelligence (AI) tools are being used to improve efficiency, mitigate risk, and enrich the customer service experience in the financial sector. Financial market swings can now be predicted with greater precision thanks to AI-driven algorithms' analysis of massive amounts of data. Automated trading systems employ AI to execute trades at fast speeds based on real-time market knowledge, optimizing returns and minimizing risks for investors. These algorithms process market data at speeds and volumes unimaginable to human traders, allowing for instantaneous judgments with far-reaching consequences for the financial markets.

Artificial intelligence (AI) has also transformed fraud detection and prevention in the financial sector. Machine learning algorithms examine user and transactional data for anomalies that might indicate fraudulent activity. By alerting financial institutions to potentially fraudulent activities in real time, AI technologies can help reduce losses and keep customers' accounts safe.

Furthermore, chatbots and virtual assistants powered by AI have revolutionized customer care in the financial sector. Customers may get fast help, have their questions answered, and have their hands held through a variety of financial processes thanks to these smart machines. These chatbots' ability to understand and reply to client inquiries in a conversational manner thanks to natural language processing (NLP) algorithms boosts customer satisfaction and engagement. Moreover, robo-advisors powered by AI evaluate customers' financial profiles and investment objectives to provide customized investment recommendations, expanding consumers' access to professional financial guidance and new investment avenues.

Supporting Smart Manufacturing Facilities and Streamlining Operations

Artificial intelligence (AI) is the driving force behind the development of "smart factories" and other innovations in the manufacturing sector. Predictive maintenance powered by artificial intelligence is a game-changer in the industrial industry. Machine learning algorithms can anticipate when machinery will fail by examining equipment data and past performance. This preventative maintenance strategy lessens the amount of money spent on repairs and increases the life of production machinery. As a result, producers can maintain high levels of productivity and meet production deadlines continuously.

Automation and robotics powered by artificial intelligence are also improving quality control and other aspects of production.

Robots with the ability to see and learn from their surroundings can do complex jobs quickly and accurately. Using their superior intelligence, these robots can check for flaws in products to guarantee they are of the highest quality. Cobots, or collaborative robots, are designed to work alongside humans in production settings to improve both productivity and worker safety. Cobots powered by AI algorithms can learn new skills and coordinate effectively with human workers to boost efficiency.

Artificial intelligence technology have been very helpful in the manufacturing sector, especially in supply chain management. Artificial intelligence systems sift through mountains of data on logistics, demand projections, and stock levels. Manufacturers may cut down on waste, save money on storage, and react quickly to shifts in demand if they use pattern recognition and optimization in inventory management. In addition, logistics optimization powered by AI provides effective transportation routes, shortening transit times and decreasing fuel consumption, both of which help to secure a sustainable future.

Accepting a Future Driven by Artificial Intelligence
The disruptive potential of AI is best demonstrated by looking at its effects in three very different sectors: healthcare, finance, and manufacturing. By embracing the power of machine learning algorithms, data analytics, and automation, businesses may achieve extraordinary levels of efficiency, accuracy, and innovation. When applied to these industries, AI not only improves current processes but also prepares the way for whole new paradigms.

Businesses must spend in areas such as research, personnel, and infrastructure in order to fully take advantage of the potential given by the widespread use of AI technology across industries. Stakeholders must also address ethical issues, data privacy worries, and workforce preparation to ensure AI advancements are adopted in a responsible and equitable manner. By fostering collaboration between technological experts, policymakers, and industry leaders, society can navigate the hurdles and maximize the benefits of the AI-driven future, ultimately producing a more efficient, interconnected, and innovative world.

Real-world case studies showcasing the impact of AI on business operations and efficiency

Artificial intelligence (AI) is changing the face of business by helping organizations become more effective, efficient, and productive than ever before. Artificial intelligence (AI) technologies are being used by businesses across all sectors to solve difficult problems and seize exciting new opportunities. This essay covers real-world case studies that graphically illustrate the transformative impact of AI on company operations and efficiency, highlighting the inventive solutions implemented by firms to stay ahead in the competitive market.

1. IBM Watson, an automated customer service solution

IBM Watson is an artificial intelligence (AI) powered cognitive computing system that has revolutionized customer service. IBM Watson uses NLP and ML algorithms to interpret user queries in real time and provide useful responses. Watson's data analysis capabilities allow it to deliver precise and individualized responses to consumer concerns, freeing up time previously spent by human customer service representatives.

IBM's collaboration with industry titan Autodesk is a shining example of such an alliance. Chatbots powered by IBM Watson were introduced at Autodesk to respond to customers' questions about the company's software and its licensing, setup, and troubleshooting. The AI-powered chatbots were accessible around-the-clock, which increased both response times and consumer satisfaction. A more effective and efficient customer service operation was achieved by automating commonly asked questions so that human agents could focus on more difficult concerns.

Ocado: Optimising Supply Chain Management

British online grocery store Ocado has automated its supply chain processes with the use of artificial intelligence. The Ocado Smart Platform (OSP) is an advanced warehouse automation technology used by Ocado. By employing AI algorithms, OSP expedites the selecting and packing of orders within the warehouse.

Robots driven by artificial intelligence are used to move around the warehouse, retrieving items from shelves and bringing them to the humans who will then pack them. Machine learning is used by these robots to improve their performance over time, allowing them to work in dynamic warehouse environments. This has allowed Ocado to reach unprecedented levels of efficiency and precision in its order fulfillment for customers. The use of AI in supply chain management has not only boosted efficiency but also cut operational costs, enabling Ocado to deliver food to clients with unprecedented speed and precision.

Third Example of Customized Service: Netflix

The popular streaming service Netflix uses AI algorithms extensively to improve the overall user experience and to make personalized content recommendations. The software takes into account the user's watching habits, preferences, and activities to provide tailored content suggestions. Netflix's use of machine learning helps the streaming service provide content that is more likely to appeal to each individual customer.

The deep learning algorithms that fuel Netflix's recommendation engine are adept at picking up on tiny trends and correlations in consumers' watching behavior. This degree of customization not only increases user retention but also benefits businesses by increasing consumer happiness. Netflix's content recommendations are regularly improved based on AI-driven insights to enhance user experience and ensure customer loyalty, ultimately leading to increased revenue.

Siemens: Fourth Step in Optimizing Production
Siemens, a multinational business, is using artificial intelligence (AI) to streamline its production procedures and increase productivity. Siemens' implementation of AI-driven predictive maintenance in its gas turbine production facilities is one such example. Artificial intelligence systems can anticipate equipment problems by evaluating data from sensors installed in turbines. Siemens is able to maximize turbine efficiency with minimal downtime thanks to this method of preventative maintenance.

Siemens uses AI in both production and quality assurance. Computer vision algorithms analyze manufactured components, identifying even the slightest faults or deviations from the specified standards. Siemens has automated this step of quality control to ensure that only high-quality items make it to market, cutting down on defects and improving production efficiency.

5. Ant Financial, Disruptor of Traditional Financial Services
Ant Financial, a subsidiary of Alibaba Group, has used artificial intelligence to completely revamp the Chinese financial services industry. Alipay is one of their top offerings, and it uses AI-powered fraud detection algorithms to identify and stop fraudulent transactions as soon as they occur. In order to identify anomalous behaviors that may be indicative of fraud, these algorithms evaluate transaction patterns, user behavior, and other characteristics. Ant Financial safeguards the safety

of its users' financial transactions and keeps their trust by preventing fraudulent transactions from being completed.

In addition, Ant Financial employs AI in the areas of credit scoring and loan disbursement. People without extensive credit histories are typically overlooked by traditional credit rating techniques. However, the artificial intelligence algorithms used by Ant Financial take into account many factors, like as one's online conduct, social connections, and shopping habits. As a result of these analyses, Ant Financial is now able to provide loans to people who were previously underserved by traditional financial institutions.

Insights into the Future of AI in Business Procedures
The real-world case studies described above provide compelling proof of the transformative influence of AI on corporate operations and efficiency. In order to remain competitive in the digital age, businesses have turned to artificial intelligence (AI) technology for help in automating customer assistance, optimizing supply chains, customizing customer experiences, improving industrial processes, and transforming financial services.

There is no limit to how AI could change the face of business as it is currently practiced. Companies that embrace AI-driven solutions are not only boosting efficiency but also obtaining a competitive edge in the market. However, incorporating AI into corporate processes successfully calls for a deliberate strategy, investment in personnel and technology, and dedication to addressing ethical considerations and data protection concerns.

In the long run, AI will be deeply embedded in how businesses function in the future. The merging of human and artificial intelligence will reshape the corporate world as companies invest in cutting-edge AI projects and seek novel applications for the technology. Business can unleash new levels of productivity, efficiency, and innovation by leveraging AI to augment human capabilities; this will pave the way for a future when AI-driven business operations are the norm, reshaping industries and the way we work and engage with technology.

The challenges and opportunities presented by AI adoption in the corporate world

Artificial intelligence (AI) has become a game-changer in the business world, presenting enterprises in all sectors with novel prospects and unprecedented problems. Machine learning and natural language processing are only two examples of AI technologies with the potential to boost productivity, encourage creativity, and facilitate better judgment. However, there are also many difficulties that arise from using AI, such as ethical worries, changes in the workplace, and data privacy concerns. This essay delves deep into the benefits and difficult obstacles presented by AI adoption in the business world.

Possibilities: Artificial Intelligence's Impact on Business
Increased Productivity and Efficiency
The potential for increased efficiency and productivity is one of the key benefits of AI adoption in the business world. Automating mundane and repetitive chores with AI can free up workers' time for more strategic and creative work. For example, chatbots and virtual assistants handle client inquiries, lowering response times and releasing human agents for complicated problem-solving. Robots powered by artificial intelligence can streamline factories' assembly lines to boost output while cutting down on mistakes.

Data-driven decision making is made possible by AI technologies because they allow firms to process and evaluate massive amounts of data. Patterns, trends, and correlations in data can be uncovered by predictive analytics and machine learning algorithms that human analysts may overlook. From improving supply chain efficiency to developing new marketing plans, everything benefits from this data-driven strategy.

Third, AI is allowing for more personalized consumer experiences by analyzing and making sense of customer data. Companies can utilize

AI to send customized marketing messages, make personalized product recommendations, and offer individualized customer service. Customer happiness is boosted, revenues are boosted, and brand loyalty is boosted because of this customization.

New ideas and approaches to doing business are sparked by the widespread implementation of AI. Applications powered by artificial intelligence are allowing for revolutionary improvements in fields like healthcare. Wealth management services are being revolutionized by AI-enabled robo-advisors. Disruptive inventions that gain market leadership and competitive advantage are typically made possible by AI adoption.

Fifthly, artificial intelligence technologies can help businesses cut expenses and improve efficiency in five key areas. For instance, automated supply chain management systems can reduce excess inventory and expedite transportation, and AI-powered predictive maintenance can reduce the likelihood of expensive equipment breakdowns. A company's bottom line and ability to compete benefit from these cuts in expenses.

The Difficulties of Artificial Intelligence Adoption
First, Concerns About Privacy And Ethics:
There are increasing ethical questions about the responsible application of increasingly complex AI systems. Concerns about algorithmic bias, data privacy, and the abuse of artificial intelligence for spying purposes have emerged as major topics of discussion. To ensure ethical usage of AI, businesses must traverse a murky moral terrain.

Second, the deployment of AI will cause a shift in the makeup of the workforce. Although AI can automate many mundane jobs, it does necessitate learning new abilities. Employees need to retrain and acquire new skills to collaborate productively with AI systems. In addition, the change could cause labor displacement, calling for reintegration and support initiatives in those instances.

Thirdly, security and data breach threats increase when organizations adopt more AI and data-driven technology. Cyberattacks and data breaches are a real threat to AI systems. Businesses must invest heavily in cybersecurity to protect their operations and protect sensitive data and AI algorithms.

4. Integration Difficulties: It can be difficult to integrate AI into preexisting organizational systems and processes. New AI technologies may not be backwards compatible with existing systems, necessitating extensive renovations. If you want things to go off without a hitch during the integration process, you'll need to plan beforehand.

Regulatory Hurdles: AI adoption is subject to developing rules, and firms must traverse a complicated landscape of laws and norms. It is essential to follow data privacy laws like Europe's General Data privacy Regulation (GDPR). To avoid legal repercussions and safeguard the company's reputation, it is critical to comprehend and abide by regulatory regulations.

Studies of Specific Applications of Artificial Intelligence and Their Results
We'll look at a few examples from the business world to show the benefits and drawbacks of implementing AI:

First Example: Automating Amazon's Distribution Centers Amazon was an early adopter of artificial intelligence for application in warehouse automation. Its Kiva robots employ artificial intelligence algorithms to streamline the distribution of goods around the warehouse. These robots can transfer shelves and merchandise to human workers, saving the time and effort required for order fulfillment. Because of this automation, Amazon is able to cut down on both delivery times and expenses.

Problem: Fears of a complete change of the workforce have been voiced as a result of the widespread use of AI-driven automation. Amazon has hired more people to keep up with its expanding business, but concerns have been raised about the impact automation would have on traditional warehouse positions. Finding a happy medium between automation and human jobs is difficult.

IBM Watson's Potential in the Healthcare Industry, Case Study 2 IBM Watson has made important contributions to the healthcare field. Clinical decision support makes use of Watson's AI capabilities to aid doctors in making diagnoses and formulating treatment strategies. Watson can analyze patient data, medical records, and research articles to deliver insights and recommendations that boost the quality of medical diagnosis and care.

Problem Ethical and privacy issues are raised by the usage of AI in healthcare. Patient data is delicate, and safeguarding its security and privacy is vital. To ensure their efficacy and safety in healthcare contexts, AI systems also need to undergo extensive testing and regular updates.

Third Case: Chatbots for Customer Service (Several Sectors)
Opportunity: Chatbots powered by artificial intelligence are being used by an increasing number of businesses across sectors, from retail to banking, to better serve their customers. These chatbots are capable of answering common client questions, recommending products, and even processing purchases. They're available around the clock, which cuts down on wait times and improves service for customers.

The difficulty in implementing chatbots is in making sure they are effective and that customers are happy with the results. In order for chatbots to properly respond to a wide variety of client requests, they need to be taught and refined over time. It's a major worry that chatbots can misinterpret or frustrate clients, which would have a negative effect on their experience.

Conclusion: Weighing the Benefits and Risks of AI Implementation

The potential gains in effectiveness, productivity, creativity, and patronage that could result from widespread use of AI in business are enormous. While there are many positive aspects, such as a transformed workforce and fewer regulations to worry about, there are also many difficult difficulties to overcome.

Companies need a deliberate strategy to AI adoption if they are to succeed in this environment. This entails investing in employee training, protecting data protection, establishing robust cybersecurity safeguards, and remaining aware about developing rules. To allay ethical worries and increase confidence among stakeholders, businesses should adopt responsible AI practices including openness, fairness, and accountability.

It is a path that involves vigilance, flexibility, and a dedication to balance opportunities with appropriate practices in order to successfully integrate AI into business processes. To continue shaping a world where AI-driven technologies coexist happily with human intelligence to fuel innovation and growth, businesses must continue to innovate and explore the potential of AI.

Chapter 3: AI in Everyday Life
How AI technologies are becoming an integral part of our daily lives

Once the purview of science fiction, Artificial Intelligence (AI) technologies are now deeply embedded in our society and shaping how we work, play, and exist in the world. Applications ranging from voice assistants to recommendation systems have incorporated AI to improve user experience, productivity, and customization. This essay delves into the far-reaching impact of AI technologies, demonstrating how they have become an inseparable part of our everyday lives and fundamentally altered our outlook on the world.

The use of AI in personal assistants such as Apple's Siri, Amazon's Alexa, Google's Assistant, and Microsoft's Cortana is one of the most obvious ways in which AI has entered our daily lives. Voice-activated, information- and reminder-giving, message-sending, and smart-home-device-controlling bots are powered by artificial intelligence. These assistants have been essential as they have improved users' ability to multitask by interpreting natural language.

Second, AI has changed the way we communicate with one another through the development of cutting-edge language processing technology. On websites, social media platforms, and mobile apps, chatbots driven by AI algorithms answer client inquiries. These bots can respond immediately, boosting responsiveness and minimizing wait times for customers. In addition, translation systems powered by AI make it easier for people of different languages to communicate with one another, increasing opportunities for international cooperation.

Third, artificial intelligence (AI) is used to improve user experiences on entertainment platforms. Netflix and Spotify utilize artificial intelligence algorithms to track what their consumers watch and listen to. Based on this information, these sites offer personalized suggestions, offering movies, TV series, or songs tailored to individual preferences. This customization not only keeps people interested, but also exposes them to fresh information they might love.

Fourth, AI is revolutionizing medicine by providing novel approaches to previously intractable problems. In order to aid in the detection and treatment of diseases, machine learning algorithms evaluate large datasets. X-ray and MRI machines that are powered by artificial intelligence can help doctors spot problems and provide more precise diagnoses. Public health responses can be improved with the use of predictive analytics driven by AI by spotting future disease outbreaks and allocating resources more wisely.

5. AI in Transportation: AI is transforming the transportation sector, particularly with the advent of autonomous vehicles. Data from sensors, cameras, and radars is processed by AI algorithms in self-driving cars so that they can safely navigate roads. The use of such vehicles could greatly improve safety, traffic flow, and access to transportation for people with physical limitations. Sustainable urban mobility is further enhanced by AI-driven transportation systems that optimize routes, minimize congestion, and enhance the effectiveness of public transportation.

The sixth application of AI is in the classroom, where it is transforming the way students learn. Adaptive algorithms allow intelligent tutoring systems to personalize lessons for each learner. Chatbots powered by AI are a fast and convenient way to get answers to questions and help with homework. Better learning outcomes and individualized instruction are possible thanks to data analytics powered by AI, which helps teachers monitor student progress, pinpoint problem areas, and adjust instruction accordingly.

7. AI in banking: The banking industry has adopted AI for numerous purposes. Algorithms powered by AI examine financial data in real

time to spot fraudulent activity, strengthening the safety of all financial dealings. Artificial intelligence (AI) is used by automated trading systems to forecast market movements and optimize investment portfolios, hence increasing traders' profits. Financial advice and investment opportunities are becoming more accessible to more people thanks to robo-advisors powered by artificial intelligence.

Future Prospects and Seamless Integration of AI
Artificial intelligence technologies are now deeply embedded in our daily lives, serving as crucial aids that increase productivity, adaptability, and ease. AI has had far-reaching and game-changing effects, from making daily life easier thanks to personal assistants to disrupting sectors like healthcare, transportation, and finance. As AI develops further, it will become ever more ingrained in our daily lives, expanding our horizons and changing our relationships with the world.

The future of AI technologies seems bright. Recent developments in areas such as NLP, CV, and RL are paving the way for new and exciting uses. The evolution of AI conversational systems is allowing for more nuanced interactions and better user experiences. Advances in artificial intelligence (AI)-powered robotic systems are being put to use in more complex and high-stakes domains like healthcare, agriculture, and disaster relief.

Ethical concerns, data privacy, and algorithmic prejudice must be addressed, however, as AI technology become more pervasive in our daily lives. For AI to have a good social impact and inspire trust among its users, its development must be conducted in an open, fair, and responsible manner.

In conclusion, artificial intelligence technologies have greatly improved many facets of our life. Their seamless integration is a testament to their versatility and promise. A future where AI technologies continue to enrich our lives and drive progress in unprecedented ways can only be guaranteed through a methodical and ethical approach to AI adoption that maximizes its benefits while limiting its problems.

A look at AI-powered applications like virtual assistants, autonomous vehicles, and smart homes

Artificial intelligence (AI) is changing the way we live, work, and interact with the world as a whole in the rapidly developing technological landscape. Virtual assistants, autonomous vehicles, and smart homes are just a few of the cutting-edge uses of AI that are already changing the way we live. This essay dives into these cutting-edge technologies, discussing their features, benefits, obstacles, and significant effects on society.

Improving Human-Computer Interaction with Virtual Assistants
Modern artificial intelligence (AI) algorithms have made virtual assistants an indispensable part of our lives. Artificial intelligence (AI) systems like Amazon's Alexa, Apple's Siri, Google Assistant, and Microsoft's Cortana use NLP and ML to interpret user input and provide appropriate responses. A new era of human-computer connection has begun with the introduction of virtual assistants into smartphones, smart speakers, and other gadgets.

Among the many features and uses offered by virtual assistants are the ability to schedule reminders, send and receive messages, make and receive phone calls, provide weather updates, and answer inquiries about a wide range of topics. They work flawlessly with other smart home gadgets, letting you command your lights, heating, and security systems with just your voice. As a result of their ability to improve the user experience and streamline interactions, virtual assistants are finding growing use in customer support applications.

Benefits:
Convenience: Virtual assistants save time and effort by eliminating the need for the user to type in questions or instructions

These AI-driven tools make it easier for people with impairments to access data and services, fostering a more accepting and equitable society.

Customization: Based on a user's history and current activity, virtual assistants can provide specific suggestions, news alerts, and other information.

Smart homes and offices benefit from virtual assistants because of how easily they interface with other AI-powered apps and smart gadgets.

Challenges:
Storing speech data gives rise to privacy worries, which in turn sparks discussions about data security and user consent in relation to the collection and use of personally identifiable information.

Concerns concerning bias in AI-powered virtual assistants' responses and recommendations, as well as users' right to privacy, are all legitimate ethical concerns.

Security: Protecting virtual assistants from cyberattacks and unauthorized access is vital to prevent malicious exploitation of these systems.

Second, How Self-Driving Cars Are Changing the Mobility Landscape
Autonomous vehicles, often known as self-driving automobiles, are revolutionizing the transportation sector. Autonomous vehicles use artificial intelligence tools like computer vision, machine learning, and sensor fusion to read road signs, avoid collisions, and make split-second judgments in response to traffic conditions. The development of autonomous cars has the potential to alter transportation, making it safer, more efficient, and accessible to a greater population.

Features and Uses: Autonomous cars use a wide variety of sensors, cameras, radar, and Lidar (Light Detection and Ranging) systems to gather information about their environment. Data from these sensors is processed by AI algorithms, allowing the car to make decisions on its own (including acceleration, braking, and steering). Ride-hailing services, public transit, logistics, and urban mobility solutions are just some of the many possible applications for these vehicles.

Benefits:
Safety: With autonomous vehicles on the road, human faults like distracted driving and poor judgment may be drastically reduced, making the roads safer for everyone.

Autonomous vehicles are more efficient because they can respond to changing traffic circumstances in real time and make judgments based on that information rather than on guesswork.

Autonomous vehicles promote accessibility for people of all abilities, including those who are disabled, elderly, or unable to drive for medical reasons.

Fuel efficiency and emissions can be improved, both contributing to environmental sustainability, through optimized travel patterns and reduced traffic congestion.

Challenges:
Safety, liability, and legal accountability must be established before the development and deployment of autonomous cars can proceed without a comprehensive regulatory framework.

Autonomous vehicles provide ethical challenges in terms of decision-making in life-or-death scenarios, such as whether or not pedestrians' lives should be prioritized over that of the vehicle's occupants in the case of an inevitable accident.

The accuracy and dependability of artificial intelligence algorithms, sensors, and communication systems must be ensured to avoid malfunctions and mishaps brought on by faulty technology.

3 Smart Homes: Designing High-Tech, Integrated Habitats

Conventional houses are upgraded to high-tech "smart homes" with the help of AI-driven automation and IoT devices. Smart homes include a network of interconnected devices and systems that allow for remote control and monitoring of things like lighting, temperature, security cameras, and appliances. In order to improve home energy efficiency, security, and comfort, AI algorithms can study human behavior and preferences.

Functionality and Applications: Smart home gadgets are equipped with sensors and communication modules that enable them to interact with each other and with users through smartphone apps or voice commands. In order to learn user patterns and provide optimal settings, AI algorithms process data from various devices. Energy management, home security, entertainment systems, and health monitoring gadgets are just some of the many uses for smart homes.

Benefits:
Smart home systems save energy use and utility costs by automatically adjusting lighting, heating, and cooling to match the schedules of whoever is home at any given time.

Safety: Security systems powered by AI can monitor the premises and immediately notify the authorities if they identify any suspicious behavior or intrusion.

With smart home automation, you can manage your heating and cooling, lighting, and media systems with just the touch of a button or the sound of your voice.

Quality of Life and Health Monitoring health metrics, sending medicine reminders, and creating a relaxing space based on one's preferences are all ways in which smart home devices can improve one's sense of well-being.

Challenges:
Interoperability: Making sure different smart home devices and platforms can communicate with one another without any hitches is crucial for avoiding technical difficulties and creating a consistent user experience.

Since smart home ecosystems gather personal information about users' habits, preferences, and activities, protecting user data and safeguarding privacy are of the utmost importance.

Safer and more widespread use of smart home technologies relies on users understanding and making the most of their devices' features, security protections, and privacy settings.

Future-Forming Connectivity and Intelligence
Virtual assistants, driverless vehicles, and smart homes show the revolutionary impact of AI technology in influencing the future of our society. In addition to improving efficiency and comfort, these apps are laying the groundwork for a more interconnected and smarter future. As these technologies continue to evolve, tackling concerns relating to privacy, ethics, security, and legislation is crucial to ensure their responsible and useful incorporation into our lives.

By working in tandem, AI and these other applications offer a future of improved human-computer connection, safer and more efficient transportation, and smart, responsive homes. Society can shape a future where technology enriches our lives, promotes diversity, and creates a more connected and intelligent world for generations to come by embracing AI-powered advancements and supporting responsible growth.

Ethical and privacy concerns related to the pervasive use of AI in society

Artificial intelligence (AI) has become a game-changer, impacting industries as diverse as medicine, banking, education, and the arts. The broad use of AI has many practical applications, but it also poses serious ethical and privacy concerns that must be carefully thought through. This essay delves into the ethical and privacy concerns raised by AI's widespread adoption in today's culture, analyzing the repercussions, dangers, and potential answers to these pressing questions.

1. Ethical Issues During the Process of Creating and Deploying AI:
Disparities in Treatment:
Large datasets used to train AI algorithms may have inherent biases. If not addressed, these prejudices can have harmful consequences that exacerbate existing inequities in society. Examples of biased algorithms in action include those used in the recruiting process, which can perpetuate sexism and racism. Careful data curation and algorithmic fairness concerns throughout development are essential for overcoming these biases.

Understanding the thought process behind an AI's decision might be difficult due to the algorithm's complexity; this is especially true for deep learning models. Problems with accountability and the ability to question AI-driven judgments are brought up by the lack of transparency. Assuring that AI systems are accountable and understood by stakeholders necessitates the establishment of transparent processes and standards, which can be aided by the use of explainable AI techniques.

Artificial intelligence (AI) systems, including driverless cars and automated weaponry, can operate independently of humans and make judgments. The morality of giving AIs the ability to make decisions needs further exploration. To avoid unexpected consequences and guarantee human oversight in crucial situations, it is crucial to establish the bounds of AI autonomy and define ethical frameworks for responsible decision-making.

Second, Data Protection Issues with AI Applications: Safeguarding Personal Information:
Artificial intelligence (AI) systems require massive volumes of data for training and functioning. It is crucial that this information be kept private and secure. Identity theft, financial fraud, and privacy violations are just some of the serious consequences that can result from unauthorized access, data breaches, or misuse of personal information. Sensitive data must be protected by using strong encryption, safe storage methods, and strict access controls.

Concerns about mass surveillance and privacy invasion are fueled by the rise of AI-powered surveillance technology like facial recognition systems and predictive analytics. Individuals' privacy is being violated by the widespread monitoring of their activities, which occurs frequently without their awareness or agreement. To prevent the misuse of surveillance technologies, it is essential to find a happy medium between protecting the public and respecting individuals' right to privacy.

Profiling and Behavioral Analysis: AI systems can analyze huge datasets to develop detailed profiles of individuals, including their interests, activities, and routines. Concerns regarding discriminatory tactics and the manipulation of consumers' decisions are raised alongside the benefits of using this data for targeted marketing and customisation. Protecting individuals against biased profiling and undue influence requires strict regulations for the gathering and use of personal data.

Reducing Privacy and Ethics Concerns
Guidelines and Regulations:
When it comes to ethical and privacy issues in AI, governments and regulatory organizations play a crucial role. Responsible advancement and rollout of AI technology can be ensured by the implementation of extensive legislation, standards, and guidelines. These frameworks need to provide developers, organizations, and consumers with explicit principles that address data protection, algorithmic transparency, accountability, and justice.

Promoting ethical AI development techniques is crucial for avoiding prejudice, achieving full openness, and retaining full accountability. Ethical AI concepts and guidelines should be adopted by organizations, with a focus on justice, explainability, and human-centered design. Assessing the ethical consequences of AI projects and encouraging responsible practices can be achieved through the use of ethical review boards and the interdisciplinary collaboration of AI professionals, ethicists, and social scientists.

Public knowledge and Education: Raising public knowledge of AI technology, their potential, and associated concerns is vital. Users who have received adequate education are better able to safeguard their personal information, comprehend the consequences of decisions influenced by AI, and advocate for ethical AI development and use. Participants in seminars and awareness campaigns can gain the knowledge they need to make educated decisions about how they interact with AI systems.

To effectively address ethical and privacy problems, it is crucial for several stakeholders, including those involved in the creation of technology, policymaking, research, and civil society organizations, to work together. Effective rules, best practices, and novel solutions can be created through open debate and the exchange of information. The inclusion of all relevant stakeholders in the decision-making process is made possible by open cooperation, which encourages a group effort to address ethical concerns.

Wrapping Up: Artificial Intelligence's Privacy and Ethical Challenges

To ensure a responsible and inclusive AI-driven future, it is crucial to address ethical and privacy concerns as AI technologies continue to permeate many areas of society. Individual rights must be safeguarded, and trust in AI systems must be fostered, by striking a balance between scientific progress and ethical considerations. Society can navigate the complexities of AI ethics and privacy, creating a future where AI benefits humanity while respecting fundamental ethical principles and privacy rights, through the implementation of robust regulations, promotion of ethical development practices, raising public awareness, and facilitation of collaboration among stakeholders. Through communal efforts and conscious implementation, the integration of AI into society can be led by ethical principles, enabling a future where AI technologies enrich human lives while preserving ethical norms and privacy standards.

Chapter 4: The Technology Behind AI
An in-depth examination of the underlying technologies and algorithms that power AI systems

Artificial intelligence (AI) is now ubiquitous, bringing revolutionary change to many fields and improving our everyday lives in countless ways. Artificial intelligence (AI) is built on a foundation of interconnected technologies and algorithms that give computers the ability to mimic human intelligence and carry out tasks that were previously thought to require human reasoning. This article provides a thorough analysis of the fundamental principles, methodologies, and developments that drive the development of artificial intelligence, as well as the underlying technology and algorithms that enable AI systems.

Artificial Intelligence's Backbone Is Machine Learning
Instructional Guidance:
An artificial intelligence model is developed using labeled datasets under the supervised learning paradigm of machine learning. These datasets consist of input-output pairs, allowing the algorithm to learn the mapping between inputs and related outputs. The algorithm optimizes its settings during training to reduce the gap between its predictions and the true labels. Image recognition, language translation, and speech recognition are just few of the many applications of this method.

Training AI models without the benefit of labels is called unsupervised learning. Unsupervised learning algorithms find patterns, structures, or correlations in the data rather than trying to predict specific outputs. Common uses of unsupervised learning include clustering and dimensionality reduction methods. Dimensionality reduction methods simplify big datasets by reducing the number of features, whereas clustering algorithms organize data into clusters based on shared characteristics.

Training artificial-intelligence agents to make successive judgments in unpredictable contexts is the primary goal of reinforcement learning. The agent acquires environmental interaction skills by doing behaviors that maximize a reward signal in the environment. To approximate difficult decision-making processes, reinforcement learning algorithms use Q-learning and deep reinforcement learning. Robotics, video games, and autonomous systems all benefit from this strategy.

Artificial Neurons: Neural Networks that Model the Human Brain

Artificial neurons, also known as perceptrons, are the backbone of neural networks and mimic the fundamental properties of their biological counterparts. To generate an output, each neuron takes in a signal, applies a weight to that signal, and then runs the resulting sum through an activation function. In a neural network, the neurons are organized into different layers, such as the input, hidden, and output layers. During training, the network's performance is improved by adjusting the weights attached to the neurons' connections with one another.

"Deep learning" is the process of teaching a neural network to recognize complex patterns and construct meaningful representations of input. When it comes to processing images and sequences of data, respectively, deep learning architectures like Convolutional Neural Networks (CNNs) and Recurrent Neural Networks (RNNs) have shown amazing effectiveness. Because of their ability to automatically extract hierarchical features, deep learning models are well-suited for applications such as image recognition, NLP, and autonomous driving.

Synonym: adversarial generative models.
To create a GAN, a generator and a discriminator neural network compete with one another. While the discriminator can tell the difference between true and fraudulent data, the generator can make its own. Application areas for adversarially trained GANs include image synthesis, style transfer, and data augmentation, among others. GANs have transformed the world of computer-generated graphics and creative content development.

Third, NLP (Natural Language Processing): A Guide to Tokenization and Text Preprocessing for Human Language:
Tokenization is the process of tokenizing text into smaller linguistic units (words, phrases, etc.) for the sake of analysis. The quality of textual data can be improved through text preparation techniques like stemming, lemmatization, and the removal of stop words. These methods reduce text's dimensionality by standardizing it, which boosts NLP models' efficacy.

When words are represented as vectors in a continuous vector space, we refer to this as a word's embedding. Word embeddings are learned by models like Word2Vec, GloVe, and FastText by taking the surrounding text into account. Word meanings and similarities can be understood by NLP models thanks to these embeddings, which encode semantic links between words. Sentiment analysis, machine translation, and named entity recognition are just few of the many applications where word embeddings are indispensable.

Recurrent Neural Networks (RNNs) and Transformers: RNNs are designed to analyze sequential input, making them appropriate for problems involving natural language sequences. Recurrent neural networks (RNNs) have the ability to capture temporal dependencies since they keep hidden states. In the Attention Is All You Need paper, the concept of a "transformer" was introduced, which greatly improved the efficiency with which NLP could capture long-range dependencies. Using self-attention processes, transformers can analyze input sequences in parallel and improve the modeling of contextual relationships.

4. Visual Data Analysis Using Computers
Deep Learning Architectures:
CNNs are a type of neural network optimized for processing data structures with regular grid patterns, such as photos and movies. Convolutional layers, pooling layers, and fully connected layers make up CNN architectures. Images are filtered using convolutional layers to pick up on details at the regional level. Downsampling occurs in the spatial dimensions of feature maps when using pooling layers. Convolutional neural networks (CNNs) play a crucial role in image classification, object detection, and picture segmentation.

YOLO (You Only Look Once) and Faster R-CNN are two examples of object detection algorithms that can locate and identify several objects in a picture. These algorithms anticipate object locations and types using region proposal networks and bounding box regression. Algorithms for segmenting photos, such as U-Net, divide images into sections defined by a single pixel. Autonomous vehicles, medical imaging, and surveillance systems all rely heavily on object detection and image segmentation.

Generative models, such as Variational Autoencoders (VAEs) and Generative Adversarial Networks (GANs), are used for picture synthesis. In order to generate new images under user control, VAEs sample from previously learnt latent spaces. As we've established, GANs are able to create convincing visuals because they train a generator and a discriminator network in an adversarial fashion. These generative models can be used in the creation of art, the enhancement of data, and the construction of lifelike avatars for use in virtual worlds.

5. Responsible Artificial Intelligence Research and Development:

Understanding and Reducing Bias:

Since AI systems will have far-reaching effects on society, it is crucial that they be open and impartial. The goal of explainable AI is to make AI models interpretable, so that interested parties can fathom the logic behind AI-based judgments. Additionally, attempts to reduce biases in training data and algorithms are vital to prevent biased outcomes and promote justice in AI applications.

Privacy and data security are moral imperatives in the field of artificial intelligence research and development. Sensitive data must be protected by using strong encryption, safe storage methods, and strict access controls. Data can be anonymized with the use of anonymization techniques and differential privacy methods, allowing for valuable analysis without compromising the privacy of individuals.

Artificial intelligence systems should prioritize user experience and accessibility. User satisfaction, ease of use, and acceptance of all users are at the forefront of human-centered design. Making AI programs accessible to people with different capacities helps ensure that nobody is left out of the conversation. Developers with a strong commitment to ethics in AI work hard to create AI systems that actually help people.

Finding Your Way Through the Maze of AI Technologies

There is a remarkable convergence of computer science, mathematics, and cognitive science in the underlying technologies and algorithms that underpin AI systems. To fully utilize the promise of AI for the greater good, it is crucial to address ethical concerns, promote fairness, and ensure openness as the field evolves. The ethical, equitable, and responsible advancement of AI systems requires a concerted effort on the part of researchers, policymakers, and industry stakeholders to negotiate the nuances of AI technologies. By accepting these ideas and developments, humanity can harness the revolutionary power of AI, pushing innovation while respecting ethical norms and creating a good impact on the world.

Machine learning, neural networks, deep learning, and natural language processing

Artificial intelligence (AI) has rapidly evolved into a game-changing tool, reshaping how we work with computers across many disciplines. Machine Learning, Neural Networks, Deep Learning, and Natural Language Processing (NLP) stand out as particularly important developments at the heart of AI's capabilities. This essay delves into the nitty-gritty of these technologies, illuminating their underlying principles, practical applications, and far-reaching implications on the future of AI-driven innovation.

Machine learning is the backbone of modern AI.
Principles and Working Definition:
Machine learning (ML) is a branch of artificial intelligence that allows computers to infer meaning from data and act accordingly without being explicitly programmed. To allow algorithms to iteratively learn from data, hence increasing their performance over time, is the core notion behind ML. ML algorithms can be broken down into three basic categories: supervised learning, unsupervised learning, and reinforcement learning.

Machine learning has many different uses, such as in autonomous vehicles, healthcare, and recommendation systems. In predictive analytics, ML algorithms examine historical data to forecast future patterns, supporting organizations in strategic decision-making. ML is used by recommendation systems on streaming sites like Netflix to make personalized recommendations to users. Medical outcomes can be improved with the use of ML models by improving disease diagnosis, drug development, and individualized therapy strategies.

Second, artificial neural networks mimic the human brain in ways that are both useful and humbling.

Neural Networks (NN) are models of artificial intelligence that mimic the way the human brain operates. In the same way as biological neurons process inputs and outputs, so too do artificial neurons, also known as perceptrons. An input layer takes in information, a set of hidden layers does the heavy lifting, and an output layer generates the model's prediction. Deep architectures in neural networks allow for the modeling of more intricate patterns and representations than their shallow counterparts.

The Power of Deep Learning to Reveal Hidden Structures

Deep Learning (DL) is a specialization of machine learning that takes advantage of neural networks with many hidden layers to discover complex patterns in large datasets. In areas like as image identification, language translation, and natural language processing, DL algorithms, especially Convolutional Neural Networks (CNNs) for image analysis and Recurrent Neural Networks (RNNs) for sequential data, have shown exceptional success. Because deep learning models can automatically discover useful features from data, feature engineering is no longer necessary.

Third, NLP facilitates human-computer interaction.

Processes for Tokenizing and Analyzing Text:

Artificial intelligence (AI)'s field of Natural Language Processing (NLP) helps computers grasp, analyze, and even create natural language. Tokenization, the process of breaking down text into smaller units like words or subwords, is the initial stage in natural language processing. Improve the quality of your textual data with text processing techniques including stemming, lemmatization, and the elimination of stop words. These preparation processes normalize text, lowering dimensionality and boosting the performance of NLP models.

Word embeddings are representations of words as vectors in a continuous vector space, and they form the basis of language models. Word embeddings are learned by models like Word2Vec, GloVe, and FastText by taking the surrounding text into account. Word meanings and similarities can be understood by NLP models thanks to these embeddings, which encode semantic links between words. Applications such as chatbots, language translation, and content creation are made possible by language models like OpenAI's GPT (Generative Pre-trained Transformer), which uses deep learning techniques to generate coherent and contextually appropriate text.

4. Developments and Issues in Artificial Intelligence Technologies

Advancements:

Models like BERT (Bidirectional Encoder Representations from Transformers) and GPT have completely changed the face of NLP thanks to recent developments in AI technology. These models make use of attention mechanisms to better understand textual linkages and capture long-range dependencies. Combining deep learning with reinforcement learning algorithms has led to significant progress in fields like game playing and autonomous systems.

Although AI has come a long way in a short amount of time, it still has some ways to go before it can be considered fully trustworthy. Transparent techniques and unbiased training data are necessary to address this critical ethical challenge and ensure fairness and prevent discrimination in AI systems. Understanding the justifications for AI-driven decisions is vital for user trust and accountability, but explainability remains a barrier, especially in complicated deep learning models.

Researchers, legislators, and industry stakeholders all need to work together on solutions to these problems.

Ethical Considerations and Future Prospects

Future Expectations:

Reinforcement learning, robots, and AI-driven creativity are just a few areas where the field of artificial intelligence (AI) could go in the future. It is anticipated that advancements in autonomous systems would be driven by reinforcement learning approaches, which will allow robots to carry out complex tasks and learn from their interactions with the environment. AI-driven creativity, evident in domains like art, music, and content creation, will continue to expand, blurring the barriers between human and machine-generated products.

As AI develops, it becomes increasingly important to think about and solve ethical concerns. Transparency, fairness, and accountability are essential to the creation of AI that can be trusted. Developers of AI systems should give high importance to neutrality of algorithms, diversity of training data, and user confidentiality. Responsible AI deployment and risk mitigation need ongoing discussions about the ethical implications of AI and the implementation of regulatory frameworks.

Insights into the Future of AI

Artificial intelligence's four pillars—Machine Learning, Neural Networks, Deep Learning, and Natural Language Processing—have propelled us into a new era of extraordinary technological progress. The way we use computers, examine data, and talk to one another has been revolutionized by these innovations. While the AI environment offers tremendous opportunity for advancement, it is essential that ethical concerns be kept in the foreground at all times.

Transparency, fairness, and accountability are cornerstones to a future where artificial intelligence (AI) technologies expand human potential, fuel innovation, and improve people's lives. In the future, artificial intelligence will coexist happily alongside human intelligence, enhancing lives and stimulating growth for decades to come, thanks to the careful development and ethical deployment of these technologies as we continue to push the boundaries of AI.

The role of data and data collection in AI development

Data is the lifeblood that drives innovation, machine learning algorithms, and the creation of AI-based intelligent systems. The learning, adapting, and decision-making abilities of AI models are limited by the quality, variety, and quantity of the data they are exposed to throughout the training process. As a result, the strengths and weaknesses of artificial intelligence are shaped in large part by the methods used to acquire data. This article goes into the complicated web of connections between data and AI research and development, discussing how data collection, curation, and application form the foundation on which AI rests.

1. Why Data Is So Vital to AI:
In the context of artificial intelligence, "data" refers to the acquired, processed, and used to train machine learning models raw information, whether structured or unstructured. In addition to text, photos, videos, audio recordings, and sensor data, data also takes on many more formats. Data is essential for AI algorithms to recognize patterns, learn from examples, and make inferences or choices. The precision, consistency, and scalability of AI models are critically dependent on the quality of the data used to train them.

Data as the Fuel for Machine Learning: Machine Learning (ML), a type of AI, relies on algorithms that learn patterns and correlations from data. For instance, supervised learning algorithms learn from input-output pairs in labeled datasets. By analyzing the labeled data, the algorithm is able to learn how to properly translate inputs to outputs. In contrast, unsupervised learning algorithms delve into unlabeled data in search of previously unknown patterns and structures. Reinforcement learning algorithms learn by interacting with an environment, receiving feedback in the form of rewards or penalties based on their behavior.

Decisions made by AI systems are data-driven since they are based on the analysis of massive amounts of data to spot patterns, outliers, and other irregularities. These discoveries help companies, academics, and government agencies make better choices, enhance existing systems, and pioneer new areas of study and practice. Making decisions based on data helps businesses get an edge in the market, provide better service to customers, and streamline internal processes.

Methods for Gathering Information:
Tools for Collecting Information:
The means of data collecting shift with the nature of the information being gathered and its final application. Opinions, attitudes, and impressions can be captured through surveys, interviews, and questionnaires used to collect qualitative data. Quantitative data is gathered through controlled experiments and surveys. In addition, technological progress has allowed for the collecting of real-time data via sensors, social media, mobile devices, and IoT (Internet of Things) devices, resulting in massive amounts of continuous data for analysis.

Difficulties in Gathering Information: Gathering information is not without its difficulties. Maintaining data reliability, completeness, and applicability is crucial. Inaccuracies and unfair AI models may come from the introduction of biases during data collection. When working with private or sensitive information, privacy concerns often emerge. The ethical problems of data gathering must be met in a way that protects individuals' privacy and rights, and this can only be done with careful thought, informed consent, and complete openness.

The Importance of Huge Data Sets for Future AI Progress:
Big Data is defined as data sets so large that they cannot be efficiently stored or retrieved using conventional database management systems. The 3Vs that define Big Data are volume (plenty of data), velocity (a lot of new data being generated quickly),

and variety (many kinds of data, both structured and unstructured). Hadoop and Spark are two examples of Big Data technologies that facilitate the storing, processing, and analysis of large datasets to reveal previously hidden insights and patterns.

The huge amounts of data stored in Big Data repositories provide ideal conditions for training sophisticated machine learning models, illustrating the inextricable nature of Big Data and machine learning. Machine learning algorithms can mine Big Data for insights, revealing patterns and relationships that can inform strategy. With the use of Big Data analytics, businesses may improve their understanding of customer behavior, market trends, and operational efficiency.

Preparing the Data and Developing the Features:
Input Data Cleaning:
Cleaning, transforming, and standardizing raw data constitute data preparation, an essential AI development phase. Preprocessing ensures that the data is in a suitable format for analysis and modeling. Improving data quality includes activities like filling in missing values, looking for outliers, and reducing noise. Inconsistencies and discrepancies in the dataset can be cleaned out during preprocessing to provide an improved and stable base for AI models.

Selecting, manipulating, or fabricating useful features from the raw data is what feature engineers do to improve the efficacy of machine learning models. Feature engineering is an art form that necessitates expertise in the relevant domain and familiarity with the issue at hand. The model's capacity to learn intricate patterns is enhanced by carefully created features that isolate the most salient aspects of the data. When the raw data lacks the necessary patterns for precise predictions, feature engineering becomes crucial.

Implications of Data Collection Ethics:

The acquisition and use of data for AI research must give careful consideration to ethical implications. To ensure individuals are aware of how their data will be used, organizations must acquire informed consent from them. It is an ethical necessity to safeguard personal information and respect people's right to privacy. In addition, privacy concerns necessitate that data be aggregated and anonymized whenever possible.

Discriminatory Outcomes from AI Models Due to Biased DataIntentional or inadvertent bias in data can have a substantial impact on AI models. To reinforce existing disparities, machine learning algorithms might prolong biases existent in historical data. The statistics may already contain societal biases such as sample error, measurement discrepancies, or incorrect definitions of key terms. Addressing prejudice involves thorough data curation, varied and representative datasets, and fairness-aware machine learning algorithms to prevent unjust outputs.

Implications for the Future of Data-Driven AI Development:
Future Tendencies:
Future progress in artificial intelligence will be closely tied to innovations in data technologies. When AI is combined with edge computing and Internet of Things devices, it will be possible to make in-the-moment decisions based on raw data. Federated learning, in which AI models are trained across distributed devices without exchanging raw data, allows for the secure use of data from several sources without compromising privacy. Businesses and organizations will be able to benefit from predictive and prescriptive analytics thanks to the development of AI-powered data analytics.

The development of AI faces difficulties in the areas of data quality, privacy, and security, despite the bright future that is predicted for the field. For AI models to perform as expected, it is crucial that their input data is accurate and trustworthy. Strong data anonymization methods and strict rules are needed to ensure people's privacy. Data security is crucial, as unauthorized access or breaches can have serious effects. Further, responsible AI development requires ongoing conversation and ethical norms to address the complexities of data acquisition and use.

Improving the Environment for Data-Driven AI

In the ever-changing field of AI, data is the bedrock upon which smart systems are constructed. Intricately woven into the process of creating AI is the interaction of many moving parts, including data collecting, preprocessing, machine learning algorithms, and ethical issues. Ethical norms, openness, and the reduction of biases must be upheld as we negotiate the complexities of this environment.

A future where artificial intelligence technologies enable society, promote innovation, and improve the quality of life is made possible by the responsible gathering, curation, and use of data. We can harness the revolutionary power of AI and create a future where intelligent systems improve human experiences, promote scientific discovery, and drive good societal change by cultivating the data-driven AI ecosystem with honesty and care. The prudent application of data will continue to be a moral and ethical necessity as we progress farther into the domains of artificial intelligence, ensuring that AI's future is one that benefits all of humanity.

Chapter 5: The Future of AI

Predictions and trends for the future of AI innovation

Artificial intelligence (AI) has quickly evolved from a specialized tool to a mainstream enabler of profound social and economic change. We are on the cusp of a new age, thus it is crucial that we take a look at the trends and forecasts that will determine the course of AI development. This essay delves into the evolution of AI technology, from the most recent discoveries in machine learning to the ethical considerations that are motivating its development, and speculates on its potential applications.

Deep Learning Advances Further:
Deep Learning, a branch of machine learning, has proven instrumental in the development of cutting-edge AI. Artificial intelligence (AI) systems will soon be able to analyze complicated patterns, comprehend nuance, and make more precise predictions thanks to future advances in deep learning algorithms. Accelerating development is anticipated in areas such as Generative Adversarial Networks (GANs) for photorealistic image production and reinforcement learning for fully autonomous decision making.

With vital applications like healthcare and banking, the 'black box' aspect of deep learning models has been a cause for concern. The goal of explainable artificial intelligence (XAI) methods is to make these models' decisions more understandable and open to scrutiny. The ability to comprehend and have faith in the judgments of more sophisticated AI systems will be crucial. Local Interpretable Model-Agnostic Explanations (LIME) and Shapley Additive Explanations (SHAP) are two examples of XAI techniques that are poised for widespread use.

The Role of Artificial Intelligence in Personalized Medicine and Drug Discovery

AI has enormous potential to improve medical treatment. With the use of machine learning algorithms, medical personnel can evaluate patient data to create treatment strategies, leading to the advent of personalized medicine. And AI is accelerating the identification of promising molecules and forecasting their efficacy in the drug discovery process, both of which are game-changing developments. New medicines and treatments could be developed thanks to the increased pace of research.

AI-powered diagnostics are improving the accuracy and efficiency of disease detection in healthcare diagnostics and imaging. Medical imaging studies, such as X-rays and MRIs, can be analyzed by machine learning algorithms for signs of cancer and neurological illnesses. This innovation may significantly alter the future of medical treatment by facilitating quicker and more accurate diagnosis and, consequently, better health outcomes for patients.

3 Artificial Intelligence and Ethics; Developing AI Morally
Ethical concerns must be given top priority as AI technologies become more pervasive in everyday life. Ensuring fairness, accountability, and transparency in AI algorithms is a developing topic. In order to promote the development of AI that does not violate human rights, regulators and organizations should adopt more stringent criteria and standards. The industry will continue to evolve in response to efforts to reduce bias in AI systems and address the repercussions of AI-based judgments on society.

There are serious privacy problems with the spread of AI. Large datasets, which may contain personally identifiable information, are frequently used by AI systems. It is a problem for society to find a happy medium between using data for AI research and development and protecting people's right to privacy. In order to protect users' privacy while still taking advantage of AI, researchers are developing new privacy-protecting methods including federated learning and homomorphic encryption.

Personalized Learning through Artificial Intelligence
Adaptive learning platforms powered by AI are revolutionizing the classroom by giving each student a unique educational experience. These technologies monitor students' performance and learning styles, modifying the curriculum in real-time to enhance learning results. Such platforms will likely be widely adopted in the future of education, as they can meet the needs of a wide range of students and improve the effectiveness of teaching and learning.

Teaching Tools Powered by Artificial Intelligence (AI): Intelligent tutoring systems and automated grading systems are just two examples of how far we've come in this area. Insights on student performance, improvement areas, and the automation of administrative work are just a few ways in which these tools help educators. Artificial intelligence (AI) in the classroom has the potential to improve instruction by creating a more stimulating setting for students to learn.

AI for Robotics and Industrial Automation:
Automation of routine tasks by robots; RPA.
Automation powered by AI is revolutionizing business processes by making it unnecessary for humans to do routine activities. RPA software, driven by AI algorithms, can automate repetitive, rule-based processes in a wide range of industries. As these technologies become more advanced, firms are likely to embrace RPA to boost operational efficiency and decrease costs.

Artificial intelligence (AI) and autonomous systems hold great potential for the future, from self-driving cars and drones to robotic butlers and secretaries. Reinforcement learning-based AI systems in particular are expanding the capabilities of these independent creatures. It is expected that autonomous systems will be widely adopted in the transportation, manufacturing, and service industries as safety measures and technology continue to advance, radically altering the way we live and work.

Sixth, Artificial Intelligence and Climate Change: Predicting and Monitoring the Environment
Artificial intelligence is a crucial tool for weather forecasting and environmental research. To forecast natural disasters, track deforestation, and evaluate air and water quality, machine learning algorithms examine massive information from satellites, weather stations, and sensors. Knowing the patterns of climate change with such precision allows for preventative measures to be taken to lessen the impact on the environment.

As the computing demands of AI algorithms rise, so does interest in creating energy-efficient AI models (thus the term "green AI"). Green AI strives to lower the carbon footprint of AI technology by optimizing algorithms, data centers, and hardware. The future of environmentally responsible AI development will be shaped by trends like studying energy-efficient AI models and using renewable energy sources for AI infrastructure.

Adopting a Responsible Approach to the AI Revolution
There's no denying that the promise of future AI innovation is thrilling, with the potential to reshape our economies, cultures, and more. But with progress comes new obligations. Artificial intelligence research and development must prioritize addressing ethical, privacy, and societal problems. To make sure these game-changing technologies actually help people as a whole, it's important to strike a balance between technological progress and moral considerations as we enter the AI revolution.

Society can navigate the AI world responsibly if it encourages interdisciplinary cooperation, prioritizes transparency, and develops ethical frameworks. Focusing on how AI can be used to improve lives, make the world a better place for everyone, and ensure a sustainable and equitable future is essential as AI continues to reshape our world. The future of AI innovation resides not merely in scientific improvements, but in the deliberate and ethical decisions we make as stewards of this new technology.

The potential societal impacts and ethical considerations of advanced AI

Artificial Intelligence (AI) has emerged as a transformational force, altering industries, improving productivity, and revolutionizing the way we live and work. Society is on the cusp of a new age as AI technologies grow at a rate never seen before. While advanced AI could have far-reaching positive effects, it also raises serious social and ethical concerns that must be examined. This essay delves into the social repercussions and ethical quandaries that come with the development of sophisticated AI, exploring the many facets of these affects.

1) The Effects of Strong AI on Society
Disruption to the economy and the loss of jobs:
Concerns about the impact that advanced AI will have on established businesses and labor markets are common. Artificial intelligence-enabled automation threatens to displace humans in many occupations. Work that consists primarily of rote actions is especially at risk. While AI-driven automation can improve company efficiency and cut costs, it also raises concerns about how the workforce will need to be retrained and reskilled to keep up with the evolving labor market.

Adopting cutting-edge AI technologies has the potential to widen already existing racial and economic divides. It's possible that some groups won't have the same level of access as others to the healthcare, education, and financial institutions that are fueled by artificial intelligence. There may be a "digital divide" if communities that lack resources or access to technology are at a disadvantage. Bridging this gap and providing equal access to AI-related possibilities are key problems for governments and society at large.

Concerns about privacy and surveillance are heightened by the fact that many cutting-edge AI systems rely on enormous databases. Facial recognition and predictive analytics are two examples of AI systems that collect personal data that could be misused without proper protections. There is an urgent need for comprehensive regulation and ethical norms to protect individuals' privacy rights against unauthorized access, data breaches, and the potential exploitation of personal data.

1.4 Decision-Making Impact: Artificial intelligence algorithms are having an ever-increasing impact on fields as diverse as law enforcement, healthcare, and finance. Unfair or biased results may be achieved, however, due to biases in the training data. Addressing these biases and maintaining openness in AI-driven decision-making are crucial to prevent propagating existing societal prejudices.

2. Moral Concerns with Cutting-Edge AI:
Accountability and Openness to Information 2.1
Ethics demand that we prioritize making AI systems accountable for their actions. It is vital to know the reasoning behind the judgments made by AI systems. Open-source projects, explainable AI, and transparent algorithms can all help increase public confidence in AI. In the case of life-or-death applications like autonomous vehicles and healthcare, companies creating AI solutions must take responsibility for the results of their systems.

The unequal distribution of resources in society can be reinforced by biased AI algorithms, as discussed in Section 2.2. Machine learning algorithms can amplify biases existing in training data, which disproportionately affects already underrepresented groups. Ethical AI research and development need inclusive and representative datasets, as well as bias-reducing fairness-aware algorithms. Fairness and the avoidance of disproportionate effects on disadvantaged communities require constant inspection and assessment.

Use of Artificial Intelligence (AI) in Conflict:
There are significant moral questions raised by the use of AI in military settings. Autonomous weapons systems, capable of making fatal decisions without human interference, offer existential concerns. Unintended consequences and violations of humanitarian law might result when human judgment is removed from battle. Strict rules and international agreements are needed to ensure the ethical use of AI in military contexts, thereby avoiding the escalation of conflicts and protecting civilian lives.

Human-AI Teamwork, Version 2.4:
The ethical implications of working together with AI systems go beyond the initial design phase. It is critical to regulate AI such that it complements human talents rather than supplants human volition. Ethical norms ought to encourage mutually beneficial partnerships in which AI aids people in performing tasks such as making decisions and becoming more creative. Ethical frameworks for AI-human cooperation should put people first, protecting their rights to privacy, agency, and respect.

Reducing Negative Social Impacts and Promoting Ethical AI Research and Development
3.1 Legal Foundations:
The advancement and use of cutting-edge AI technologies must be governed by solid regulatory frameworks. Guidelines, standards, and accountability procedures must be established through a coordinated effort by governments and international agencies. Data privacy, fairness, openness, and accountability are all important topics that should be addressed in

regulations. Compliance with ethical standards and societal norms can be verified by auditing and certifying AI systems.

To address the societal effects and ethical concerns of advanced AI, interdisciplinary collaboration is essential (3.2). It is imperative that ethicists, policymakers, engineers, and social scientists collaborate to foresee the repercussions of AI developments. The ethical repercussions of AI projects can be evaluated, and appropriate development techniques can be recommended, via ethical review committees made up of specialists from a variety of professions.

Education and outreach efforts to increase the general public's understanding of artificial intelligence (AI) and its applications, consequences, and responsibilities are essential. Teaching people what AI is and how it works helps them make more educated decisions and gives them more agency in defining AI policy. Further, preparing the next generation with the knowledge and critical thinking abilities needed to traverse the difficulties of AI-driven societies can be accomplished by encouraging digital literacy and ethical education in schools and colleges.

3.4 Industry Self-Regulation: Industry stakeholders have a crucial role in shaping the ethical landscape of AI development. Organizations conducting research and conducting business should self-regulate in accordance with established ethical standards. Transparency in AI research, ethical impact evaluations, and ethical standards of conduct can all help encourage responsible innovation. In order to develop best practices and ethical benchmarks for AI technologies, business leaders, academics, and civil society organizations should work together.

The Ethical Challenges of Cutting-Edge AI, Part 4

There are many moral and social considerations to be made as we move forward on the path to realizing AI's full potential. Ethical considerations must be given top priority as we move into new area to ensure that AI advancements are for the greater good of humanity. This delicate balance between scientific progress and social responsibility can be achieved by encouraging interdisciplinary collaboration, imposing strict rules, and raising public awareness.

The future of human-machine interactions will be heavily influenced by the development of ethical AI, therefore it's not only a technological necessity. To create a future where technology improves human well-being, protects human rights, and promotes a just and equitable society, it is crucial to adhere to ethical standards in the creation and implementation of cutting-edge artificial intelligence. The moral compass that has guided AI development thus far must hold true if we are to arrive at a time when cutting-edge AI tools can improve people's lives without compromising the core principles that give us our humanity.

The importance of responsible AI development and the need for regulation

Now more than ever, artificial intelligence (AI) is transforming many sectors of our economy and society. As its impact increases, the need for ethical advancements in artificial intelligence has become critical. Ethical, fair, transparent, and accountable development of AI entails making intelligent systems that help people while minimizing harm to society. Comprehensive regulation becomes more and more necessary as the AI environment develops. This essay dives into the necessity for regulatory frameworks that defend ethical practices and societal well-being, and it examines the significance of responsible AI development.

Foundations and Principles for Responsible AI Development
1.1 Moral Concerns:
The foundation of ethical AI development is ethics. AI systems can harm individual privacy, influence decision-making processes, and perpetuate biases. Ethical AI is AI that does no harm, protects people's privacy, and upholds other basic human rights. Trust among users and stakeholders is increased when AI engineers adhere to ethical principles such as fairness, transparency, and responsibility.

Artificial intelligence (AI) algorithms can perpetuate existing societal biases if they are trained on biased data, resulting in unfair decisions. Techniques for identifying and correcting algorithmic biases are essential for responsible AI development. The goal of techniques like adversarial debiasing and fairness-aware machine learning is to build AI systems that are fair to all people, regardless of their gender, color, or other identifying characteristics.

Transparency in AI systems guarantees that the decision-making processes may be comprehended and interpreted in a meaningful way. Users are better able to trust and be held accountable for the decisions made by AI systems when those systems can explain their thought processes. Transparent AI models allow stakeholders, including legislators, to analyze the underlying mechanisms, ensuring that judgments accord with ethical standards and social values.

Responsible AI development relies heavily on a system of human accountability and oversight (see section 1.4). Having developers, organizations, and end users all take some degree of accountability for an AI system's results is essential. Particularly in the realms of medicine and the law, where human discretion is indispensable, human oversight is essential. Decisions shouldn't be delegated to algorithms without ethical inspection, therefore it's important to strike a balance between AI's automation capabilities and human monitoring.

Why We Need Rules for Artificial Intelligence:
Regulation plays a crucial role in ensuring that AI technology follow ethical guidelines. 2.1 Ensuring Ethical Standards. Regulations establish legal limitations and repercussions for unethical activities, whereas ethical norms give a framework for behavior. Ethical AI development can be established by regulations that spell out what is and is not allowed in the field, providing developers and organizations with a road map for their AI projects.

Concerns about privacy and data security are amplified by the fact that many AI applications rely on enormous datasets. Regulations can require strict data protection procedures, guaranteeing the proper handling of private and sensitive information. Safeguarding individuals' right to privacy, data anonymization, encryption, and secure storage techniques can lessen the impact of data breaches.

Regulations can include instructions for mitigating bias and discrimination in AI systems (see Section 2.3). By enforcing criteria for varied and representative datasets, legislation can limit the risk of biased algorithms. Algorithms that are naturally fair and unbiased can be developed with the help of legislation that encourage research and development in this area of machine learning

Building public trust in AI requires that its systems be open and accountable to its users. Developers may be required to explain AI-based conclusions as a result of transparency requirements imposed by regulations. In addition, rules can set up channels of responsibility, making businesses answerable for the results of their AI projects. In order to encourage ethical AI development and use, legal frameworks might establish culpability and accountability norms.

Third, issues and factors to consider while regulating AI:
AI technologies are complex and rapidly developing, making it difficult to draft legislation that can keep up with these changes. The policymakers must find a middle ground between rigid rules and room for creativity. Understanding the complexities of AI developments and designing appropriate legislation requires continuous collaboration between policymakers and engineers.

Since AI research and development occurs on a global scale, international cooperation is essential for regulatory efforts. Global regulatory harmonization maintains uniformity and eliminates regulatory arbitrage, in which businesses take advantage of disparities in regulatory requirements between countries. Through international cooperation, best practices can be shared and a coordinated strategy can be developed to meet the ethical concerns faced by AI technologies.

3.3 Accountability and Ethical Supervision:
Ethical systems for monitoring compliance with regulations are required for their effective implementation. The ethical conformity of AI technologies can be monitored by independent regulatory organizations and ethical review boards. Continuously evaluating the effects of AI technologies requires accountability mechanisms like audits and assessments. Effective ethical monitoring requires both open reporting and regular assessments.

The Final Thought: How Government Can Foster Responsible AI Development

Harnessing the potential for social benefit while minimizing risks associated with AI technology requires their responsible development. The foundation of ethical AI development is found in fairness, openness, and accountability. The ethical climate is heavily influenced by regulations, which provide a legal framework to direct AI efforts by developers, companies, and users.

There is an urgent need for all-encompassing and flexible rules as AI spreads throughout more and more industries. In order to create legislation that strike a balance between innovation and ethics, policymakers, technologists, ethicists, and the general public must work together. An ethical, equitable, and responsible future where intelligent systems benefit human lives can be fostered through responsible AI development and effective regulation. Assuring that the AI revolution evolves in a way that is consistent with human values, encourages ethical behavior, and furthers social well-being requires embracing the synergy between responsible AI development and regulation.

conclusion

AI Innovations: Transforming Industries and Lives

Artificial Intelligence (AI) is a shining example of innovation in the broad terrain of technical progress; it ushers in a new era of opportunities and alters the way we view many sectors and our own lives. As we make our way through the complex maze of AI developments, it becomes clear that this revolutionary technology is more than a fad; it is a transformative force that is changing the fundamental foundations of our societies, economy, and everyday lives. In this investigation of AI's impact on numerous sectors, we have witnessed its tremendous influence on healthcare, education, manufacturing, entertainment, and beyond. As we reach the end of our journey, it's important to consider the many ways in which AI is changing the world and ushering in a future that was previously thought to be science fiction.

Artificial intelligence has made important strides in the medical field. Accurate disease diagnosis and individualized treatment strategies are now possible thanks to the combination of machine learning algorithms and predictive analytics. Wearable devices and health monitoring systems have been made possible by AI-driven technology, giving people more control over their own health. The divide between patients and healthcare practitioners has been closed through innovations such as remote patient monitoring, telemedicine, and virtual health assistants.

AI has revolutionized the classroom by making education more flexible, engaging, and accessible to students of all backgrounds. Learning patterns are analyzed by intelligent tutoring systems so that lessons can be customized for each student. Artificial intelligence (AI)-powered online learning systems and virtual classrooms make for more interactive and immersive classroom experiences. Assessment technologies powered by AI also give teachers information into their students' growth, which can lead to more precise teaching and learning.

The introduction of AI technologies has caused a sea change in the manufacturing sector. Automation and robotics, backed by AI algorithms, have improved production processes, enhancing efficiency and precision. Equipment downtime is reduced and resource usage is maximized thanks to predictive maintenance algorithms. Supply chain management systems with artificial intelligence (AI) optimize stock levels, improve demand forecasts, and cut down on overhead expenses. Smart factories powered by AI-driven systems transform the manufacturing industry by facilitating seamless collaboration between humans and machines.

Even the entertainment industry has been revolutionized by advancements in artificial intelligence. Artificial intelligence (AI) algorithms are used by streaming platforms to learn about individual users so that they can provide more relevant and engaging content recommendations. Characters and settings enabled by artificial intelligence in video games make for an engaging and interactive experience. Creative professionals, such as artists and filmmakers, can benefit from AI-powered content production tools. For the sake of future generations, deep learning algorithms have even been used to colorize and restore old videos.

Further applications of AI are being made in other areas, such as the economy, agriculture, transportation, and environmental protection. Artificial intelligence algorithms study market behavior and trade data to help investors make better predictions and predictions. Precision farming methods powered by AI help farmers maximize their harvests while also reducing their impact on the environment and saving valuable resources. Autonomous vehicles, led by AI systems, are revolutionizing the transportation business, promising safer and more efficient mobility options. Artificial intelligence is used by environmental scientists for data analysis, climate change tracking, and the development of conservation and sustainable development plans.

Despite AI's bright future, there are still significant ethical concerns and cultural obstacles to overcome. Issues of bias, privacy, and accountability must be carefully considered for the appropriate development and implementation of AI technologies. Fair and impartial AI algorithms are essential to preventing the reinforcement of societal biases. Strong legislation and ethical frameworks are necessary to protect personal privacy in the era of pervasive data collecting. Furthermore, careful debate and open regulations are required due to the ethical implications of AI in decision-making processes like autonomous vehicles and criminal justice systems.

In conclusion, advancements in AI are certainly changing industries and people's daily lives in previously unimaginable ways. Unprecedented opportunities have arisen as a result of the coming together of data, algorithms, and computer power. As we stand at the threshold of this technological revolution, it is vital for society to embrace AI with a mix of enthusiasm and vigilance. Harnessing AI's full potential while tackling the issues that come with its rapid growth requires nurturing a culture of innovation and ethical awareness.

The development of AI and its subsequent widespread use is a remarkable example of human creativity and the unrelenting pursuit of knowledge. Working together in the future will be critical for scholars, legislators, business leaders, and the general public. Harnessing the transformative power of AI, we can build a future where industries thrive, lives are enriched, and the limits of what is possible continue to expand by cultivating a collaborative ecosystem that encourages innovation, upholds ethical standards, and prioritizes the well-being of humanity.

www.ingramcontent.com/pod-product-compliance
Lightning Source LLC
LaVergne TN
LVHW010604070526
838199LV00063BA/5066